Zoom In on Materials

Glass

Andrea Rivera

abdopublishing.com

Published by Abdo Zoom™, PO Box 398166, Minneapolis, Minnesota 55439. Copyright © 2018 by Abdo Consulting Group, Inc. International copyrights reserved in all countries. No part of this book may be reproduced in any form without written permission from the publisher. Abdo Zoom™ is a trademark and logo of Abdo Consulting Group, Inc.

Printed in the United States of America, North Mankato, Minnesota
042017
092017

Cover Photo: Jodi Jacobson/iStockphoto
Interior Photos: Jodi Jacobson/iStockphoto, 1; Ivana Star/iStockphoto, 4; iStockphoto, 5, 11; Tomas Works/iStockphoto, 6; Jean Gill/iStockphoto, 7; Benoit Daoust/Shutterstock Images, 8–9; Maren Winter/Shutterstock Images, 12; Diyana Dimitrova/Shutterstock Images, 13; Kaca Studio/iStockphoto, 14; Bill Oxford/iStockphoto, 15; Cylon Photo/iStockphoto, 17; Karel Noppe/iStockphoto, 18; Bruno Haver/iStockphoto, 19; Vladimir Wrangel/Shutterstock Images, 21

Editor: Brienna Rossiter
Series Designer: Madeline Berger
Art Direction: Dorothy Toth

Publishers Cataloging-in-Publication Data
Names: Rivera, Andrea, author.
Title: Glass / by Andrea Rivera.
Description: Minneapolis, MN : Abdo Zoom, 2018. | Series: Materials |
    Includes bibliographical references and index.
Identifiers: LCCN 2017931133 | ISBN 9781532120305 (lib. bdg.) |
    ISBN 9781614797418 (ebook) | ISBN 9781614797975 (Read-to-me ebook)
Subjects: LCSH: Glass--Juvenile literature.
Classification: DDC 620.1/44--dc23
LC record available at http://lccn.loc.gov/2017931133

Table of Contents

Glass is a material.
It is made from
sand and **minerals**.

Glass is used to make many things.
Light bulbs are made from glass.
So are windows.

Furnaces melt sand and minerals. This creates a very hot liquid.

The liquid is cooled quickly.
Glass forms.

Technology

Heating glass makes it soft and easy to shape. Adding chemicals can change the color of glass. The chemicals can also make the glass stronger.

Bullet-resistant glass has layers of clear plastic. They go between layers of glass. A bullet can go through the first layer of glass. But the other layers stop it.

Glassblowers use a **hollow** pipe. They dip it in melted glass.

Then they blow into the pipe.
Air goes inside the glass.
It makes the glass expand.

Other tools shape and cut the glass. Some glassblowers make dishes or vases.

Others make decorations.

Glass can be recycled. Broken glass is melted. It is used to make more glass. This helps save energy.

Recycling one bottle saves enough energy to run a computer for 25 minutes.

Recycling three bottles saves more energy. The computer could run for 75 minutes.

Key Stats

- People have used glass for many years. The oldest glass objects are beads from ancient Egypt. They were made around 2,500 BCE.

- Glass is used to make many things. Computer screens, cooking dishes, and jewelry can be made from glass.

- Some buildings have stained glass windows. Pieces of colored glass are joined together to make pictures.

Glossary

decoration - something added to an object or place to make it look better.

expand - to stretch or get bigger.

furnace - a chamber where fuel is burned to produce heat.

hollow - having space inside.

mineral - a substance that forms naturally under the ground.

recycled - used again or used to make something new.

Booklinks

For more information on glass, please visit abdobooklinks.com

Zoom In on STEAM!

Learn even more with the Abdo Zoom STEAM database. Check out abdozoom.com for more information.

Index